MW00893725

Prayer Journal
and Bible Study

A Devotional Guide for Prayer and Bible Study

By Debra Chapoton

Copyright © 2021 by Debra Chapoton

Cover by Boone Patchard

All rights reserved.

No part of this book may be reproduced in any form or by any electronic or mechanical means, including information storage and retrieval systems, without written permission from the author, except for the use of brief quotations in a book review.

ISBN: 9798782999261

Imprint: Independently published

Other Christian Books in this series:

Prayer Journal and Bible Study in the Gospels
Prayer Journal and Bible Study for Men
Guided Prayer Journal for Women
Crossing the Scriptures
35 Lessons from the Book of Psalms
Teens in the Bible
Moms in the Bible
Animals in the Bible
Old Testament Lessons in the Bible
New Testament Lessons in the Bible
Prayer Journal and Bible Study
(Spanish edition: Diario de Oraciones Para Mujeres y Estudio de la Biblia)

This journal belongs to

_____

How to use this journal:

Fill in the starter page with what you are most thankful for this minute, what you need the Lord's help with tomorrow, and what your spiritual goal is for the week. Here's a list of possible goals:

- To be humble
- To trust God
- To forgive others
- To be grateful
- To have faith
- To be kind
- To spread love
- To be happy
- To straighten priorities
- To make better choices
- To be more empathetic
- To practice tolerance
- To study the Bible
- To pray throughout the day
- To control temper
- To have patience
- To memorize a verse
- To let go of a vice
- To be mindful of God
- To promote peace
- To restore a friendship
- To reflect Jesus
- To confess my sins
- To worship more
- To show compassion
- To teach Scripture to someone
- To share the Gospel
- To guard my heart (avoid bad words, situations, people)

Read the suggested Bible chapter. Fill in the guided worksheet. Try to memorize the focus verse or at least rewrite it onto a post-it note or 3 x 5 card.

Pray daily according to the prompter and your notes.

There's no better habit than reading the Bible every single day! May God bless you.

What I'm most grateful for today:

_____

Lord, help me tomorrow to:

_____

My spiritual goal this week:

_____

Date _____

Prayer Prompter: **Dear God, help me look forward to my time with You each and every day.**

Friends I need to pray for:

_____   _____   _____

_____   _____   _____

Things on my heart:

_____   _____   _____

Answers to prayer:

_____

_____

Personal requests:

_____

_____

Today's Scripture reading: Hebrews 4 (focus on verse 12)

What stood out to me in this reading: _____

_____

_____

_____

_____

How I can praise God and be a better Christian today and tomorrow:

_____

_____

Things God has laid on my heart today:

_____

_____

I praise You God for answering my prayers. Help me trust You more.

What I'm most grateful for today:

_____

Lord, help me tomorrow to:

_____

My spiritual goal this week:

_____

Date _____

Prayer Prompter: **Dear God, help me look forward to my time with You each and every day.**

Friends I need to pray for:

_____ _____ _____

_____ _____ _____

Things on my heart:

_____ _____ _____

Answers to prayer:

_____

_____

Personal requests:

_____

_____

Today's Scripture: Psalm 33 (focus on verse 4)

What stood out to me in this reading: _____

_____

_____

_____

How I can praise God and be a better Christian today and tomorrow:

_____

_____

Things God has laid on my heart today:

_____

_____

I praise You God for all good things. Help me know You more.

What I'm most grateful for today:

_____

Lord, help me tomorrow to:

_____

My spiritual goal this week:

_____

Date _____

Prayer Prompter: **Dear God, give me a clear purpose today.**

Friends I need to pray for:

_____   _____   _____

_____   _____   _____

Things on my heart:

_____   _____   _____

Answers to prayer:

_____

_____

Personal requests:

_____

_____

Today's Scripture: Matthew 4 (focus on verse 4)

What stood out to me in this reading: _____

_____

_____

_____

_____

How I can praise God and be a better Christian today and tomorrow:

_____

_____

Things God has laid on my heart today:

_____

_____

I praise You God for listening to my prayers. Help me trust You more.

What I'm most grateful for today:

_____

Lord, help me tomorrow to:

_____

My spiritual goal this week:

_____

Date _____

Prayer Prompter: **Dear God, I pray for my neighbor _____ today.**

Friends I need to pray for:

_____   _____   _____

_____   _____   _____

Things on my heart:

_____   _____   _____

Answers to prayer:

_____

_____

Personal requests:

_____

_____

Today's Scripture: Psalm 12 (focus on verse 6)

What stood out to me in this reading: _____

_____

_____

_____

_____

How I can praise God and be a better Christian today and tomorrow:

_____

_____

Things God has laid on my heart today:

_____

_____

I praise You God for answering my prayers. Help me trust You more.

What I'm most grateful for today:

_____

Lord, help me tomorrow to:

_____

My spiritual goal this week:

_____

Date _____

Prayer Prompter: **Dear God, I pray for peace today.**

Friends I need to pray for:

_____   _____   _____

_____   _____   _____

Things on my heart:

_____   _____   _____

Answers to prayer:

_____

_____

Personal requests:

_____

_____

Today's Scripture: John 8 (focus on verse 32)

What stood out to me in this reading: _____

_____

_____

_____

_____

How I can praise God and be a better Christian today and tomorrow:

_____

_____

Things God has laid on my heart today:

_____

_____

I praise You God for hearing my prayers. Help me learn your Word.

What I'm most grateful for today:

_____

Lord, help me tomorrow to:

_____

My spiritual goal this week:

_____

Date _____

Prayer Prompter: **Dear God, I especially pray for** _____ **today.**

Friends I need to pray for:

_____   _____   _____

_____   _____   _____

Things on my heart:

_____   _____   _____

Answers to prayer:

_____

_____

Personal requests:

_____

_____

Today's Scripture: Matthew 7 (focus on verse 24)

What stood out to me in this reading: _____

_____

_____

_____

_____

How I can praise God and be a better Christian today and tomorrow:

_____

_____

Things God has laid on my heart today:

_____

_____

I thank You Lord for answering my prayers. Help me through this day.

What I'm most grateful for today:

_____

Lord, help me tomorrow to:

_____

My spiritual goal this week:

_____

Date _____

Prayer Prompter: **Dear God, thank you for _____, and _____, and _____.**

Friends I need to pray for:

_____   _____   _____

_____   _____   _____

Things on my heart:

_____   _____   _____

Answers to prayer:

_____

_____

Personal requests:

_____

_____

Today's Scripture: James 1 (focus on verse 22)

What stood out to me in this reading: _____

_____

_____

_____

_____

How I can praise God and be a better Christian today and tomorrow:

_____

_____

Things God has laid on my heart today:

_____

_____

I praise You Father God for answering my prayers.

What I'm most grateful for today:

_____

Lord, help me tomorrow to:

_____

My spiritual goal this week:

_____

Date _____

Prayer Prompter: **Dear God, thank you for Your free gift of salvation through Your Son.**

Friends I need to pray for:

_____   _____   _____

_____   _____   _____

Things on my heart:

_____   _____   _____

Answers to prayer:

_____

_____

Personal requests:

_____

_____

Today's Scripture: 2nd Timothy 3 (focus on verse 16)

What stood out to me in this reading: _____

_____

_____

_____

_____

How I can praise God and be a better Christian today and tomorrow:

_____

_____

Things God has laid on my heart today:

_____

_____

I praise You God Almighty for all You do for me.

What I'm most grateful for today:

_____

Lord, help me tomorrow to:

_____

My spiritual goal this week:

_____

Date _____

Prayer Prompter: **Dear God, help me let go of my plans and follow Yours.**

Friends I need to pray for:

_____   _____   _____

_____   _____   _____

Things on my heart:

_____   _____   _____

Answers to prayer:

_____

_____

Personal requests:

_____

_____

Today's Scripture: Psalm 119 (focus on verse 9)

What stood out to me in this reading: _____

_____

_____

_____

_____

How I can praise God and be a better Christian today and tomorrow:

_____

_____

Things God has laid on my heart today:

_____

_____

I praise You God of the universe for hearing my prayers. Help me love You more.

What I'm most grateful for today:

_____

Lord, help me tomorrow to:

_____

My spiritual goal this week:

_____

Date _____

Prayer Prompter: **Dear God, thank you for** _____ **in my life.**

Friends I need to pray for:

_____   _____   _____

_____   _____   _____

Things on my heart:

_____   _____   _____

Answers to prayer:

_____

_____

Personal requests:

_____

_____

_____

Today's Scripture: Proverbs 30 (focus on verse 5)

What stood out to me in this reading: _____

_____

_____

_____

_____

How I can praise God and be a better Christian today and tomorrow:

_____

_____

Things God has laid on my heart today:

_____

_____

I praise You Lord above for answering my prayers. Help me trust You more.

What I'm most grateful for today:

_____

Lord, help me tomorrow to:

_____

My spiritual goal this week:

_____

Date _____

Prayer Prompter: **Dear God, give me patience today.**

Friends I need to pray for:

_____   _____   _____

_____   _____   _____

Things on my heart:

_____   _____   _____

Answers to prayer:

_____

_____

Personal requests:

_____

_____

Today's Scripture: Genesis 16 (focus on verse 13)

What stood out to me in this reading: _____

_____

_____

_____

_____

How I can praise God and be a better Christian today and tomorrow:

_____

_____

Things God has laid on my heart today:

_____

_____

Thank You God for answering my prayers. Help me pray selflessly.

What I'm most grateful for today:

_____

Lord, help me tomorrow to:

_____

My spiritual goal this week:

_____

Date _____

Prayer Prompter: **Dear God, thank You for always being here for me.**

Friends I need to pray for:

_____   _____   _____

_____   _____   _____

Things on my heart:

_____   _____   _____

Answers to prayer:

_____

_____

Personal requests:

_____

_____

Today's Scripture: Psalm 145 (focus on verse 9)

What stood out to me in this reading: _____

_____

_____

_____

How I can praise God and be a better Christian today and tomorrow:

_____

_____

Things God has laid on my heart today:

_____

_____

I praise You God for sending Your Son. Help me trust in Him.

What I'm most grateful for today:

_____

Lord, help me tomorrow to:

_____

My spiritual goal this week:

_____

Date _____

Prayer Prompter: **Dear God, draw my family closer to You.**

Friends I need to pray for:

_____   _____   _____

_____   _____   _____

Things on my heart:

_____   _____   _____

Answers to prayer:

_____

_____

Personal requests:

_____

_____

Today's Scripture: Isaiah 43 (focus on verse 5)

What stood out to me in this reading: _____

_____

_____

_____

_____

How I can praise God and be a better Christian today and tomorrow:

_____

_____

Things God has laid on my heart today:

_____

_____

I praise You God for answering my prayers. Help me trust You more.

What I'm most grateful for today:

_____

Lord, help me tomorrow to:

_____

My spiritual goal this week:

_____

Date _____

Prayer Prompter: **Dear God, be with those who are grieving todayi.**

Friends I need to pray for:

_____   _____   _____

_____   _____   _____

Things on my heart:

_____   _____   _____

Answers to prayer:

_____

_____

Personal requests:

_____

_____

_____

Today's Scripture: Matthew 28 (focus on verse 20)

What stood out to me in this reading: _____

_____

_____

_____

_____

How I can praise God and be a better Christian today and tomorrow:

_____

_____

Things God has laid on my heart today:

_____

_____

I praise You Father for listening to my pleas. Thank You.

What I'm most grateful for today:

_____

Lord, help me tomorrow to:

_____

My spiritual goal this week:

_____

Date _____

Prayer Prompter: **Dear God, please be with our leaders and guide them in their decisions.**

Friends I need to pray for:

_____   _____   _____

_____   _____   _____

Things on my heart:

_____   _____   _____

Answers to prayer:

_____

_____

Personal requests:

_____

_____

_____

Today's Scripture: Numbers 6 (focus on verse 24)

What stood out to me in this reading: _____

_____

_____

_____

_____

How I can praise God and be a better Christian today and tomorrow:

_____

_____

Things God has laid on my heart today:

_____

_____

I praise You God in all things. Help me see You in all things.

What I'm most grateful for today:

_____

Lord, help me tomorrow to:

_____

My spiritual goal this week:

_____

Date _____

Prayer Prompter: **Dear God, be with our brothers and sisters in Christ.**

Friends I need to pray for:

_____   _____   _____

_____   _____   _____

Things on my heart:

_____   _____   _____

Answers to prayer:

_____

_____

Personal requests:

_____

_____

Today's Scripture: Proverbs 2 (focus on verse 6)

What stood out to me in this reading: _____

_____

_____

_____

_____

How I can praise God and be a better Christian today and tomorrow:

_____

_____

Things God has laid on my heart today:

_____

_____

I praise You God for answering my prayers. Help me trust You more.

What I'm most grateful for today:

_____

Lord, help me tomorrow to:

_____

My spiritual goal this week:

_____

Date _____

Prayer Prompter: **Dear God, bring physical and spiritual healings to those who need it today.**

Friends I need to pray for:

_____   _____   _____

_____   _____   _____

Things on my heart:

_____   _____   _____

Answers to prayer:

_____

_____

Personal requests:

_____

_____

_____

Today's Scripture: Genesis 1 (focus on verse 1)

What stood out to me in this reading: _____

_____

_____

_____

_____

How I can praise God and be a better Christian today and tomorrow:

_____

_____

Things God has laid on my heart today:

_____

_____

I praise You God for answering my prayers. Help me have more faith.

What I'm most grateful for today:

_____

Lord, help me tomorrow to:

_____

My spiritual goal this week:

_____

Date _____

Prayer Prompter: **Dear God, please be with my loved ones at work, school, and home.**

Friends I need to pray for:

_____   _____   _____

_____   _____   _____

Things on my heart:

_____   _____   _____

Answers to prayer:

_____

_____

Personal requests:

_____

_____

Today's Scripture: Psalm 19 (focus on verse 1)

What stood out to me in this reading: _____

_____

_____

_____

_____

How I can praise God and be a better Christian today and tomorrow:

_____

_____

Things God has laid on my heart today:

_____

_____

I praise You God for answering my prayers. Help me accept Your answers.

What I'm most grateful for today:

_____

Lord, help me tomorrow to:

_____

My spiritual goal this week:

_____

Date _____

Prayer Prompter: **Dear God, protect us from evil.**

Friends I need to pray for:

_____   _____   _____

_____   _____   _____

Things on my heart:

_____   _____   _____

Answers to prayer:

_____

_____

Personal requests:

_____

_____

Today's Scripture: Hebrews 13 (focus on verse 8)

What stood out to me in this reading: _____

_____

_____

_____

How I can praise God and be a better Christian today and tomorrow:

_____

_____

Things God has laid on my heart today:

_____

_____

I praise You God for hearing my prayers. Help me be patient in waiting on Your answers.

What I'm most grateful for today:

_____

Lord, help me tomorrow to:

_____

My spiritual goal this week:

_____

Date _____

Prayer Prompter: **Dear God, please draw** _____ **closer to Jesus.**

Friends I need to pray for:

_____   _____   _____

_____   _____   _____

Things on my heart:

_____   _____   _____

Answers to prayer:

_____

_____

Personal requests:

_____

_____

_____

Today's Scripture: Exodus 14 (focus on verse 14)

What stood out to me in this reading: _____

_____

_____

_____

How I can praise God and be a better Christian today and tomorrow:

_____

_____

Things God has laid on my heart today:

_____

_____

I praise You Father, Son, and Holy Spirit.

What I'm most grateful for today:

_____

Lord, help me tomorrow to:

_____

My spiritual goal this week:

_____

Date _____

Prayer Prompter: **Dear God, I pray for our church leaders and each member.**

Friends I need to pray for:

_____   _____   _____

_____   _____   _____

Things on my heart:

_____   _____   _____

Answers to prayer:

_____

_____

Personal requests:

_____

_____

Today's Scripture: Psalm 46 (focus on verse 1)

What stood out to me in this reading: _____

_____

_____

_____

How I can praise God and be a better Christian today and tomorrow:

_____

_____

Things God has laid on my heart today:

_____

_____

Thank You Lord for answering my prayers.

What I'm most grateful for today:

_____

Lord, help me tomorrow to:

_____

My spiritual goal this week:

_____

Date _____

Prayer Prompter: **Dear Heavenly Father, thank you for all my blessings.**

_____   _____   _____

_____   _____   _____

Things on my heart:

_____   _____   _____

Answers to prayer:

_____

_____

Personal requests:

_____

_____

Today's Scripture: Romans 10 (focus on verse 12)

What stood out to me in this reading: _____

_____

_____

_____

_____

How I can praise God and be a better Christian today and tomorrow:

_____

_____

Things God has laid on my heart today:

_____

_____

I praise You God for the wind and the rain, for all nature that is in Your control.

What I'm most grateful for today:

_____

Lord, help me tomorrow to:

_____

My spiritual goal this week:

_____

Date _____

Prayer Prompter: **Dear Heavenly Father, thank You for my home.**

Friends I need to pray for:

_____   _____   _____

_____   _____   _____

Things on my heart:

_____   _____   _____

Answers to prayer:

_____

_____

Personal requests:

_____

_____

_____

Today's Scripture: Isaiah 40 (focus on verse 28)

What stood out to me in this reading: _____

_____

_____

_____

_____

How I can praise God and be a better Christian today and tomorrow:

_____

_____

Things God has laid on my heart today:

_____

_____

I praise You God for all Your blessings. Help me see the smallest gifts.

What I'm most grateful for today:

_____

Lord, help me tomorrow to:

_____

My spiritual goal this week:

_____

Date _____

Prayer Prompter: **Dear Lord, help me sing praises to You in my heart all day long.**

Friends I need to pray for:

_____   _____   _____

_____   _____   _____

Things on my heart:

_____   _____   _____

Answers to prayer:

_____

_____

Personal requests:

_____

_____

Today's Scripture: Matthew 28 (focus on verse 6)

What stood out to me in this reading: _____

_____

_____

_____

How I can praise God and be a better Christian today and tomorrow:

_____

_____

Things God has laid on my heart today:

_____

_____

I praise You Lord. How majestic is Your name in all the earth.

What I'm most grateful for today:

_____

Lord, help me tomorrow to:

_____

My spiritual goal this week:

_____

Date _____

Prayer Prompter: **Dear Father God, help me love** _____.

Friends I need to pray for:

_____   _____   _____

_____   _____   _____

Things on my heart:

_____   _____   _____

Answers to prayer:

_____

_____

Personal requests:

_____

_____

Today's Scripture: John 14 (focus on verses 1 and 6)

What stood out to me in this reading: _____

_____

_____

_____

_____

How I can praise God and be a better Christian today and tomorrow:

_____

_____

Things God has laid on my heart today:

_____

_____

I praise You God that You accept me as I am.

What I'm most grateful for today:

_____

Lord, help me tomorrow to:

_____

My spiritual goal this week:

_____

Date _____

Prayer Prompter: **Dear Lord, help me dwell on that which is good and put away evil thoughts.**

Friends I need to pray for:

_____   _____   _____

_____   _____   _____

Things on my heart:

_____   _____   _____

Answers to prayer:

_____

_____

Personal requests:

_____

_____

Today's Scripture: John 10 (focus on verse 30)

What stood out to me in this reading: _____

_____

_____

_____

_____

How I can praise God and be a better Christian today and tomorrow:

_____

_____

Things God has laid on my heart today:

_____

_____

Thank You Lord for the air I breathe, the sustenance You provide, and for my family.

What I'm most grateful for today:

_____

Lord, help me tomorrow to:

_____

My spiritual goal this week:

_____

Date _____

Prayer Prompter: **Dear Heavenly Father, thank You for Your everlasting love.**

Friends I need to pray for:

_____   _____   _____

_____   _____   _____

Things on my heart:

_____   _____   _____

Answers to prayer:

_____

_____

Personal requests:

_____

_____

_____

Today's Scripture: Matthew 28 (focus on verse 20)

What stood out to me in this reading: _____

_____

_____

_____

_____

How I can praise God and be a better Christian today and tomorrow:

_____

_____

Things God has laid on my heart today:

_____

_____

I praise You God for hearing my prayers. Help me trust You more.

What I'm most grateful for today:

_____

Lord, help me tomorrow to:

_____

My spiritual goal this week:

_____

Date _____

Prayer Prompter: **Dear God, thank You for Your everlasting grace.**

Friends I need to pray for:

_____   _____   _____

_____   _____   _____

Things on my heart:

_____   _____   _____

Answers to prayer:

_____

_____

Personal requests:

_____

_____

_____

Today's Scripture: Corinthians 3 (focus on verse 17)

What stood out to me in this reading: _____

_____

_____

_____

_____

How I can praise God and be a better Christian today and tomorrow:

_____

_____

Things God has laid on my heart today:

_____

_____

I praise You God for answering my prayers.

What I'm most grateful for today:

_____

Lord, help me tomorrow to:

_____

My spiritual goal this week:

_____

Date _____

Prayer Prompter: **Dear Father, thank You for Your everlasting mercy.**

Friends I need to pray for:

_____   _____   _____

_____   _____   _____

Things on my heart:

_____   _____   _____

Answers to prayer:

_____

_____

Personal requests:

_____

_____

Today's Scripture: Romans 5 (focus on verse 8)

What stood out to me in this reading: _____

_____

_____

_____

_____

How I can praise God and be a better Christian today and tomorrow:

_____

_____

Things God has laid on my heart today:

_____

_____

I praise You God for setting the moon and stars in the sky and giving us the light of the sun.

What I'm most grateful for today:

_____

Lord, help me tomorrow to:

_____

My spiritual goal this week:

_____

Date _____

Prayer Prompter: **Dear God, please protect our nation's children.**

Friends I need to pray for:

_____   _____   _____

_____   _____   _____

Things on my heart:

_____   _____   _____

Answers to prayer:

_____

_____

Personal requests:

_____

_____

Today's Scripture: John 3 (focus on verses 16, 17, and 18)

What stood out to me in this reading: _____

_____

_____

_____

How I can praise God and be a better Christian today and tomorrow:

_____

_____

Things God has laid on my heart today:

_____

_____

I thank You Lord for Your Son, Jesus, the Christ, the only Savior.

What I'm most grateful for today:

_____

Lord, help me tomorrow to:

_____

My spiritual goal this week:

_____

Date _____

Prayer Prompter: **Dear God, help me go about my day with a sweet and humble spirit.**

Friends I need to pray for:

_____   _____   _____

_____   _____   _____

Things on my heart:

_____   _____   _____

Answers to prayer:

_____

_____

Personal requests:

_____

_____

Today's Scripture: John 16 (focus on verse 33)

What stood out to me in this reading: _____

_____

_____

_____

How I can praise God and be a better Christian today and tomorrow:

_____

_____

Things God has laid on my heart today:

_____

_____

I praise You God for answering my prayers. Help me trust You more.

What I'm most grateful for today:

_____

Lord, help me tomorrow to:

_____

My spiritual goal this week:

_____

Date _____

Prayer Prompter: **Dear God, help me accept Your answers to my prayers.**

Friends I need to pray for:

_____   _____   _____

_____   _____   _____

Things on my heart:

_____   _____   _____

Answers to prayer:

_____

_____

Personal requests:

_____

_____

Today's Scripture: Galatians 5 (focus on verses 22 and 23)

What stood out to me in this reading: _____

_____

_____

_____

_____

How I can praise God and be a better Christian today and tomorrow:

_____

_____

Things God has laid on my heart today:

_____

_____

I praise You God for my health. I am grateful.

What I'm most grateful for today:

_____

Lord, help me tomorrow to:

_____

My spiritual goal this week:

_____

Date _____

Prayer Prompter: **Dear God, help me be humble today.**

Friends I need to pray for:

_____   _____   _____

_____   _____   _____

Things on my heart:

_____   _____   _____

Answers to prayer:

_____

_____

Personal requests:

_____

_____

Today's Scripture reading: 1st Thessalonians 5 (focus on verse 17)

What stood out to me in this reading: _____

_____

_____

_____

How I can praise God and be a better Christian today and tomorrow:

_____

_____

Things God has laid on my heart today:

_____

_____

I praise You Lord Jesus for dying for me.

What I'm most grateful for today:

_____

Lord, help me tomorrow to:

_____

My spiritual goal this week:

_____

Date _____

Prayer Prompter: **Dear God, thank You for sending Your Son to die for my sins.**

Friends I need to pray for:

_____   _____   _____

_____   _____   _____

Things on my heart:

_____   _____   _____

Answers to prayer:

_____

_____

Personal requests:

_____

_____

Today's Scripture: Philippians 4 (focus on verse 4)

What stood out to me in this reading: _____

_____

_____

_____

_____

How I can praise God and be a better Christian today and tomorrow:

_____

_____

Things God has laid on my heart today:

_____

_____

Thank You, Jesus. You are my Lord.

What I'm most grateful for today:

_____

Lord, help me tomorrow to:

_____

My spiritual goal this week:

_____

Date _____

Prayer Prompter: **Dear God, please be with** _____ **who is having a difficult time.**

Friends I need to pray for:

_____   _____   _____

_____   _____   _____

Things on my heart:

_____   _____   _____

Answers to prayer:

_____

_____

Personal requests:

_____

_____

Today's Scripture: Psalm 150 (focus on verse 6)

What stood out to me in this reading: _____

_____

_____

_____

_____

How I can praise God and be a better Christian today and tomorrow:

_____

_____

Things God has laid on my heart today:

_____

_____

I praise You God for answering my prayers. Help me tell others of Your love.

What I'm most grateful for today:

_____

Lord, help me tomorrow to:

_____

My spiritual goal this week:

_____

Date _____

Prayer Prompter: **Dear God, help me seek You with all my heart.**

Friends I need to pray for:

_____   _____   _____

_____   _____   _____

Things on my heart:

_____   _____   _____

Answers to prayer:

_____

_____

Personal requests:

_____

_____

Today's Scripture: 1st Peter 5 (focus on verse 7)

What stood out to me in this reading: _____

_____

_____

_____

_____

How I can praise God and be a better Christian today and tomorrow:

_____

_____

Things God has laid on my heart today:

_____

_____

I praise You God for making me. Help me accept myself.

What I'm most grateful for today:

_____

Lord, help me tomorrow to:

_____

My spiritual goal this week:

_____

Date _____

Prayer Prompter: **Dear Lord, please heal** _____ **who suffers with** _____.

Friends I need to pray for:

_____   _____   _____

_____   _____   _____

Things on my heart:

_____   _____   _____

Answers to prayer:

_____

_____

Personal requests:

_____

_____

Today's Scripture: Acts 16 (focus on verse 31)

What stood out to me in this reading: _____

_____

_____

_____

_____

How I can praise God and be a better Christian today and tomorrow:

_____

_____

Things God has laid on my heart today:

_____

_____

Thank You God for answering my prayers. Help me pray throughout this day.

What I'm most grateful for today:

_____

Lord, help me tomorrow to:

_____

My spiritual goal this week:

_____

Date _____

Prayer Prompter: **Dear Lord, please be with the refugees from _____.**

Friends I need to pray for:

_____   _____   _____

_____   _____   _____

Things on my heart:

_____   _____   _____

Answers to prayer:

_____

_____

Personal requests:

_____

_____

Today's Scripture: Acts 16 (focus on verse 31)

What stood out to me in this reading: _____

_____

_____

_____

_____

How I can praise God and be a better Christian today and tomorrow:

_____

_____

Things God has laid on my heart today:

_____

_____

I praise You God for hearing my prayers. Help me pray more honestly.

What I'm most grateful for today:

_____

Lord, help me tomorrow to:

_____

My spiritual goal this week:

_____

Date _____

Prayer Prompter: **Dear Lord, thank You for all I have. All my blessings are from You.**

Friends I need to pray for:

_____   _____   _____

_____   _____   _____

Things on my heart:

_____   _____   _____

Answers to prayer:

_____

_____

Personal requests:

_____

_____

Today's Scripture: Matthew 5 (focus on verse 14)

What stood out to me in this reading: _____

_____

_____

_____

How I can praise God and be a better Christian today and tomorrow:

_____

_____

Things God has laid on my heart today:

_____

_____

Help me Lord today in all I do.

What I'm most grateful for today:

_____

Lord, help me tomorrow to:

_____

My spiritual goal this week:

_____

Date _____

Prayer Prompter: **Dear Almighty God, help me memorize Your Holy Word.**

Friends I need to pray for:

_____   _____   _____

_____   _____   _____

Things on my heart:

_____   _____   _____

Answers to prayer:

_____

_____

Personal requests:

_____

_____

_____

Today's Scripture: Ecclesiastes 12 (focus on verse 13)

What stood out to me in this reading: _____

_____

_____

_____

_____

How I can praise God and be a better Christian today and tomorrow:

_____

_____

Things God has laid on my heart today:

_____

_____

Help me Lord to speak Your truth to others.

What I'm most grateful for today:

_____

Lord, help me tomorrow to:

_____

My spiritual goal this week:

_____

Date _____

Prayer Prompter: **Dear Lord, today I am most thankful for** _____.

Friends I need to pray for:

_____   _____   _____

_____   _____   _____

Things on my heart:

_____   _____   _____

Answers to prayer:

_____

_____

Personal requests:

_____

_____

Today's Scripture: 1st Corinthians 10 (focus on verse 31)

What stood out to me in this reading: _____

_____

_____

_____

_____

How I can praise God and be a better Christian today and tomorrow:

_____

_____

Things God has laid on my heart today:

_____

_____

_____

Lord, help me be a witness for You.

What I'm most grateful for today:

_____

Lord, help me tomorrow to:

_____

My spiritual goal this week:

_____

Date _____

Prayer Prompter: **Dear God, bless the marriage of _____ and _____.**

Friends I need to pray for:

_____   _____   _____

_____   _____   _____

Things on my heart:

_____   _____   _____

Answers to prayer:

_____

_____

Personal requests:

_____

_____

Today's Scripture: Acts 5 (focus on verse 29)

What stood out to me in this reading: _____

_____

_____

_____

_____

How I can praise God and be a better Christian today and tomorrow:

_____

_____

Things God has laid on my heart today:

_____

_____

I praise You God for hearing my prayers. Help me.

What I'm most grateful for today:

_____

Lord, help me tomorrow to:

_____

My spiritual goal this week:

_____

Date _____

Prayer Prompter: **Dear God, help me get control of** _____.

Friends I need to pray for:

_____   _____   _____

_____   _____   _____

Things on my heart:

_____   _____   _____

Answers to prayer:

_____

_____

Personal requests:

_____

_____

_____

Today's Scripture: Isaiah 26 (focus on verse 4)

What stood out to me in this reading: _____

_____

_____

_____

_____

How I can praise God and be a better Christian today and tomorrow:

_____

_____

Things God has laid on my heart today:

_____

_____

I praise You God for always listening to my prayers. Help me listen to You.

What I'm most grateful for today:

_____

Lord, help me tomorrow to:

_____

My spiritual goal this week:

_____

Date _____

Prayer Prompter: **Dear Lord, I confess I need** _____.

Friends I need to pray for:

_____   _____   _____

_____   _____   _____

Things on my heart:

_____   _____   _____

Answers to prayer:

_____

_____

Personal requests:

_____

_____

_____

Today's Scripture: Joshua 1 (focus on verse 9)

What stood out to me in this reading: _____

_____

_____

_____

_____

How I can praise God and be a better Christian today and tomorrow:

_____

_____

Things God has laid on my heart today:

_____

_____

Lord, open my eyes and ears to Your Word. Give me wisdom in discerning Truth.

What I'm most grateful for today:

_____

Lord, help me tomorrow to:

_____

My spiritual goal this week:

_____

Date _____

Prayer Prompter: **Dear God Almighty, I thank You that You are still on the throne.**

Friends I need to pray for:

_____   _____   _____

_____   _____   _____

Things on my heart:

_____   _____   _____

Answers to prayer:

_____

_____

Personal requests:

_____

_____

_____

Today's Scripture: Deuteronomy 6 (focus on verse 5)

What stood out to me in this reading: _____

_____

_____

_____

_____

How I can praise God and be a better Christian today and tomorrow:

_____

_____

Things God has laid on my heart today:

_____

_____

I praise You God for answering my prayers. Open my heart to others.

What I'm most grateful for today:

_____

Lord, help me tomorrow to:

_____

My spiritual goal this week:

_____

Date _____

Prayer Prompter: **Dear God, I pray for** _____ **who doesn't know You.**

Friends I need to pray for:

_____   _____   _____

_____   _____   _____

Things on my heart:

_____   _____   _____

Answers to prayer:

_____

_____

Personal requests:

_____

_____

_____

Today's Scripture: Ephesians 6 (focus on verse 1)

What stood out to me in this reading: _____

_____

_____

_____

How I can praise God and be a better Christian today and tomorrow:

_____

_____

Things God has laid on my heart today:

_____

_____

I praise You God for hearing my prayers. Help me love You more.

What I'm most grateful for today:

_____

Lord, help me tomorrow to:

_____

My spiritual goal this week:

_____

Date _____

Prayer Prompter: **Dear Jesus, help me look forward to my time with You each and every day.**

Friends I need to pray for:

_____   _____   _____

_____   _____   _____

Things on my heart:

_____   _____   _____

Answers to prayer:

_____

_____

Personal requests:

_____

_____

_____

Today's Scripture: 2nd Timothy 1 (focus on verse 7)

What stood out to me in this reading: _____

_____

_____

_____

_____

How I can praise God and be a better Christian today and tomorrow:

_____

_____

Things God has laid on my heart today:

_____

_____

I praise You God for giving us Your Word. Help me learn more.

What I'm most grateful for today:

_____

Lord, help me tomorrow to:

_____

My spiritual goal this week:

_____

Date _____

Prayer Prompter: **Dear Jesus, create in me a clean heart.**

Friends I need to pray for:

_____   _____   _____

_____   _____   _____

Things on my heart:

_____   _____   _____

Answers to prayer:

_____

_____

Personal requests:

_____

_____

Today's Scripture: Ephesians 4 (focus on verse 32)

What stood out to me in this reading: _____

_____

_____

_____

_____

How I can praise God and be a better Christian today and tomorrow:

_____

_____

Things God has laid on my heart today:

_____

_____

I praise You Jesus for answering my prayers. Help me depend on You more.

What I'm most grateful for today:

_____

Lord, help me tomorrow to:

_____

My spiritual goal this week:

_____

Date _____

Prayer Prompter: **Dearest Jesus, I love You. Please be with me today. Thank You.**

Friends I need to pray for:

_____   _____   _____

_____   _____   _____

Things on my heart:

_____   _____   _____

Answers to prayer:

_____

_____

Personal requests:

_____

_____

Today's Scripture: Colossians 3 (focus on verse 20)

What stood out to me in this reading: _____

_____

_____

_____

_____

How I can praise God and be a better Christian today and tomorrow:

_____

_____

Things God has laid on my heart today:

_____

_____

I praise You God for answering my prayers. Help me trust You more.

What I'm most grateful for today:

_____

Lord, help me tomorrow to:

_____

My spiritual goal this week:

_____

Date _____

Prayer Prompter: **Dear God, give me wisdom and discernment.**

Friends I need to pray for:

_____   _____   _____

_____   _____   _____

Things on my heart:

_____   _____   _____

Answers to prayer:

_____

_____

Personal requests:

_____

_____

_____

Today's Scripture: Matthew 22 (focus on verse 39)

What stood out to me in this reading: _____

_____

_____

_____

_____

How I can praise God and be a better Christian today and tomorrow:

_____

_____

Things God has laid on my heart today:

_____

_____

I praise You God in all things. Help me pray in Your will.

What I'm most grateful for today:

_____

Lord, help me tomorrow to:

_____

My spiritual goal this week:

_____

Date _____

Prayer Prompter: **Dear God, I pray for selflessness to serve those around me.**

Friends I need to pray for:

_____   _____   _____

_____   _____   _____

Things on my heart:

_____   _____   _____

Answers to prayer:

_____

_____

Personal requests:

_____

_____

Today's Scripture: Proverbs 14 (focus on verse 5)

What stood out to me in this reading: _____

_____

_____

_____

How I can praise God and be a better Christian today and tomorrow:

_____

_____

Things God has laid on my heart today:

_____

_____

I praise You God. Help me praise You in public.

What I'm most grateful for today:

_____

Lord, help me tomorrow to:

_____

My spiritual goal this week:

_____

Date _____

Prayer Prompter: **Dear God, I pray for a strong, wise mind, and clean thoughts.**

Friends I need to pray for:

_____   _____   _____

_____   _____   _____

Things on my heart:

_____   _____   _____

Answers to prayer:

_____

_____

Personal requests:

_____

_____

Today's Scripture: Matthew 7 (focus on verse 1)

What stood out to me in this reading: _____

_____

_____

_____

_____

How I can praise God and be a better Christian today and tomorrow:

_____

_____

Things God has laid on my heart today:

_____

_____

I praise You God. Let the words of my mouth honor You.

What I'm most grateful for today:

_____

Lord, help me tomorrow to:

_____

My spiritual goal this week:

_____

Date _____

Prayer Prompter: **Dear Lord, please be with my pastor and the church staff.**

Friends I need to pray for:

_____   _____   _____

_____   _____   _____

Things on my heart:

_____   _____   _____

Answers to prayer:

_____

_____

Personal requests:

_____

_____

_____

Today's Scripture: Luke 6 (focus on verse 31)

What stood out to me in this reading: _____

_____

_____

_____

_____

How I can praise God and be a better Christian today and tomorrow:

_____

_____

Things God has laid on my heart today:

_____

_____

I praise You God for answering my prayers. Help me trust You more.

What I'm most grateful for today:

_____

Lord, help me tomorrow to:

_____

My spiritual goal this week:

_____

Date _____

Prayer Prompter: **Dear God, lift the bitterness from my heart and help me forgive others.**

Friends I need to pray for:

_____   _____   _____

_____   _____   _____

Things on my heart:

_____   _____   _____

Answers to prayer:

_____

_____

Personal requests:

_____

_____

Today's Scripture: Exodus 29 (focus on verse 46)

What stood out to me in this reading: _____

_____

_____

_____

How I can praise God and be a better Christian today and tomorrow:

_____

_____

Things God has laid on my heart today:

_____

_____

Dearest Lord, thank You for this day.

What I'm most grateful for today:

_____

Lord, help me tomorrow to:

_____

My spiritual goal this week:

_____

Date _____

Prayer Prompter: **Dear God, help me have a deeper trust in You.**

Friends I need to pray for:

_____   _____   _____

_____   _____   _____

Things on my heart:

_____   _____   _____

Answers to prayer:

_____

_____

Personal requests:

_____

_____

_____

Today's Scripture: Leviticus 18 (focus on verse 22)

What stood out to me in this reading: _____

_____

_____

_____

_____

How I can praise God and be a better Christian today and tomorrow:

_____

_____

Things God has laid on my heart today:

_____

_____

Dear Heavenly Father, lead me in Your paths today.

What I'm most grateful for today:

_____

Lord, help me tomorrow to:

_____

My spiritual goal this week:

_____

Date _____

Prayer Prompter: **Dear God, give me a deeper understanding of who You are.**

Friends I need to pray for:

_____   _____   _____

_____   _____   _____

Things on my heart:

_____   _____   _____

Answers to prayer:

_____

_____

Personal requests:

_____

_____

Today's Scripture: Numbers 14 (focus on verses 20 and 21)

What stood out to me in this reading: _____

_____

_____

_____

_____

How I can praise God and be a better Christian today and tomorrow:

_____

_____

Things God has laid on my heart today:

_____

_____

_____

Dear Father, You are the most powerful, most wonderful, most awesome God.

What I'm most grateful for today:

_____

Lord, help me tomorrow to:

_____

My spiritual goal this week:

_____

Date _____

Prayer Prompter: **Dear God, give me a hunger for Your Word.**

Friends I need to pray for:

_____   _____   _____

_____   _____   _____

Things on my heart:

_____   _____   _____

Answers to prayer:

_____

_____

Personal requests:

_____

_____

Today's Scripture: Jeremiah 29 (focus on verse 11)

What stood out to me in this reading: _____

_____

_____

_____

_____

How I can praise God and be a better Christian today and tomorrow:

_____

_____

Things God has laid on my heart today:

_____

_____

I praise You for another day. May I keep You, Lord, always in my thoughts.

What I'm most grateful for today:

_____

Lord, help me tomorrow to:

_____

My spiritual goal this week:

_____

Date _____

Prayer Prompter: **Dear God, give us Sabbath rest. Help us keep the day holy, unto You.**

Friends I need to pray for:

_____   _____   _____

_____   _____   _____

Things on my heart:

_____   _____   _____

Answers to prayer:

_____

_____

Personal requests:

_____

_____

Today's Scripture: Nahum 1 (focus on verse 7)

What stood out to me in this reading: _____

_____

_____

_____

_____

How I can praise God and be a better Christian today and tomorrow:

_____

_____

Things God has laid on my heart today:

_____

_____

Guide me this day, Lord. Help me trust You more.

What I'm most grateful for today:

_____

Lord, help me tomorrow to:

_____

My spiritual goal this week:

_____

Date _____

Prayer Prompter: **Dear Jesus, thank You, thank You, thank You.**

Friends I need to pray for:

_____   _____   _____

_____   _____   _____

Things on my heart:

_____   _____   _____

Answers to prayer:

_____

_____

Personal requests:

_____

_____

Today's Scripture: Psalm 34 (focus on verse 18)

What stood out to me in this reading: _____

_____

_____

_____

How I can praise God and be a better Christian today and tomorrow:

_____

_____

Things God has laid on my heart today:

_____

_____

I praise You God for answering my prayers. Be with me today.

What I'm most grateful for today:

_____

Lord, help me tomorrow to:

_____

My spiritual goal this week:

_____

Date _____

Prayer Prompter: **Dear God, I pray for the Jews who don't know Jesus is the Messiah.**

Friends I need to pray for:

_____   _____   _____

_____   _____   _____

Things on my heart:

_____   _____   _____

Answers to prayer:

_____

_____

Personal requests:

_____

_____

Today's Scripture: Psalm 55 (focus on verse 22)

What stood out to me in this reading: _____

_____

_____

_____

_____

How I can praise God and be a better Christian today and tomorrow:

_____

_____

Things God has laid on my heart today:

_____

_____

I praise You God for hearing my prayers. Give me the answers I need.

What I'm most grateful for today:

_____

Lord, help me tomorrow to:

_____

My spiritual goal this week:

_____

Date _____

Prayer Prompter: **Dear Heavenly Father, please give strength to the weak.**

Friends I need to pray for:

_____   _____   _____

_____   _____   _____

Things on my heart:

_____   _____   _____

Answers to prayer:

_____

_____

Personal requests:

_____

_____

_____

Today's Scripture: Zephaniah 3 (focus on verse 17)

What stood out to me in this reading: _____

_____

_____

_____

_____

How I can praise God and be a better Christian today and tomorrow:

_____

_____

Things God has laid on my heart today:

_____

_____

I praise You God for listening to my prayers. I trust You will give me the answers I should have.

What I'm most grateful for today:

_____

Lord, help me tomorrow to:

_____

My spiritual goal this week:

_____

Date _____

Prayer Prompter: **Dear Lord, comfort those who feel rejected.**

Friends I need to pray for:

_____   _____   _____

_____   _____   _____

Things on my heart:

_____   _____   _____

Answers to prayer:

_____

_____

Personal requests:

_____

_____

Today's Scripture: Revelation 1 (focus on verse 3)

What stood out to me in this reading: _____

_____

_____

_____

_____

How I can praise God and be a better Christian today and tomorrow:

_____

_____

Things God has laid on my heart today:

_____

_____

Lord Almighty, be with me this week.

What I'm most grateful for today:

_____

Lord, help me tomorrow to:

_____

My spiritual goal this week:

_____

Date _____

Prayer Prompter: **Dear Lord, help me love the unlovable.**

Friends I need to pray for:

_____   _____   _____

_____   _____   _____

Things on my heart:

_____   _____   _____

Answers to prayer:

_____

_____

Personal requests:

_____

_____

Today's Scripture: Revelation 21 (focus on verse 4)

What stood out to me in this reading: _____

_____

_____

_____

_____

How I can praise God and be a better Christian today and tomorrow:

_____

_____

Things God has laid on my heart today:

_____

_____

Lord, thank You for being with me every moment.

What I'm most grateful for today:

_____

Lord, help me tomorrow to:

_____

My spiritual goal this week:

_____

Date _____

Prayer Prompter: **Dear God, guide my way this day.**

Friends I need to pray for:

_____   _____   _____

_____   _____   _____

Things on my heart:

_____   _____   _____

Answers to prayer:

_____

_____

Personal requests:

_____

_____

Today's Scripture: Mark 16 (focus on verse 16)

What stood out to me in this reading: _____

_____

_____

_____

_____

How I can praise God and be a better Christian today and tomorrow:

_____

_____

Things God has laid on my heart today:

_____

_____

God in Heaven, I praise You. Bless us, O Lord.

What I'm most grateful for today:

_____

Lord, help me tomorrow to:

_____

My spiritual goal this week:

_____

Date _____

Prayer Prompter: **Dear God, help me hold my tongue when I should.**

Friends I need to pray for:

_____   _____   _____

_____   _____   _____

Things on my heart:

_____   _____   _____

Answers to prayer:

_____

_____

Personal requests:

_____

_____

Today's Scripture: Mark 12 (focus on verse 30)

What stood out to me in this reading: _____

_____

_____

_____

_____

How I can praise God and be a better Christian today and tomorrow:

_____

_____

Things God has laid on my heart today:

_____

_____

How I need You Lord! Be with me each day.

What I'm most grateful for today:

_____

Lord, help me tomorrow to:

_____

My spiritual goal this week:

_____

Date _____

Prayer Prompter: **Dear Father God, make me Your disciple in every situation.**

Friends I need to pray for:

_____   _____   _____

_____   _____   _____

Things on my heart:

_____   _____   _____

Answers to prayer:

_____

_____

Personal requests:

_____

_____

Today's Scripture: Luke 9 (focus on verse 23)

What stood out to me in this reading: _____

_____

_____

_____

How I can praise God and be a better Christian today and tomorrow:

_____

_____

Things God has laid on my heart today:

_____

_____

Help me love others as You love us, dear Lord.

What I'm most grateful for today:

_____

Lord, help me tomorrow to:

_____

My spiritual goal this week:

_____

Date _____

Prayer Prompter: **Dear Lord, give the courage and the words to tell others of Your love.**

Friends I need to pray for:

_____   _____   _____

_____   _____   _____

Things on my heart:

_____   _____   _____

Answers to prayer:

_____

_____

Personal requests:

_____

_____

Today's Scripture: 2nd John 1 (focus on verse 5)

What stood out to me in this reading: _____

_____

_____

_____

_____

How I can praise God and be a better Christian today and tomorrow:

_____

_____

Things God has laid on my heart today:

_____

_____

Lord of all, I thank You for all my many blessings.

What I'm most grateful for today:

_____

Lord, help me tomorrow to:

_____

My spiritual goal this week:

_____

Date _____

Prayer Prompter: **Dear Father, open my eyes to what You'd have me do and say today.**

Friends I need to pray for:

_____   _____   _____

_____   _____   _____

Things on my heart:

_____   _____   _____

Answers to prayer:

_____

_____

Personal requests:

_____

_____

Today's Scripture: 3rd John 1 (focus on verse 11)

What stood out to me in this reading: _____

_____

_____

_____

How I can praise God and be a better Christian today and tomorrow:

_____

_____

Things God has laid on my heart today:

_____

_____

I praise You God for hearing my prayers. Help me love You more.

What I'm most grateful for today:

_____

Lord, help me tomorrow to:

_____

My spiritual goal this week:

_____

Date _____

Prayer Prompter: **Dear Jesus, please heal** _____.

Friends I need to pray for:

_____   _____   _____

_____   _____   _____

Things on my heart:

_____   _____   _____

Answers to prayer:

_____

_____

Personal requests:

_____

_____

Today's Scripture: Daniel 3 (focus on verse 17)

What stood out to me in this reading: _____

_____

_____

_____

_____

How I can praise God and be a better Christian today and tomorrow:

_____

_____

Things God has laid on my heart today:

_____

_____

I praise You God. Help me trust You this day.

What I'm most grateful for today:

_____

Lord, help me tomorrow to:

_____

My spiritual goal this week:

_____

Date _____

Prayer Prompter: **Dear God, hold** _____ **in Your loving arms.**

Friends I need to pray for:

_____   _____   _____

_____   _____   _____

Things on my heart:

_____   _____   _____

Answers to prayer:

_____

_____

Personal requests:

_____

_____

Today's Scripture: Jude (focus on verse 20)

What stood out to me in this reading: _____

_____

_____

_____

How I can praise God and be a better Christian today and tomorrow:

_____

_____

Things God has laid on my heart today:

_____

_____

Thank You for Jesus, Lord. Help me spread the Gospel.

What I'm most grateful for today:

_____

Lord, help me tomorrow to:

_____

My spiritual goal this week:

_____

Date _____

Prayer Prompter: **Dear Heavenly Father, thank You for another day.**

Friends I need to pray for:

_____   _____   _____

_____   _____   _____

Things on my heart:

_____   _____   _____

Answers to prayer:

_____

_____

Personal requests:

_____

_____

Today's Scripture: Titus 1 (focus on verse 2)

What stood out to me in this reading: _____

_____

_____

_____

_____

How I can praise God and be a better Christian today and tomorrow:

_____

_____

Things God has laid on my heart today:

_____

_____

_____

Be with me this day, Lord, as I reach out to others.

What I'm most grateful for today:

_____

Lord, help me tomorrow to:

_____

My spiritual goal this week:

_____

Date _____

Prayer Prompter: **Dear Lord, please mend the broken and heal the sick.**

Friends I need to pray for:

_____   _____   _____

_____   _____   _____

Things on my heart:

_____   _____   _____

Answers to prayer:

_____

_____

Personal requests:

_____

_____

Today's Scripture reading (up to me): _____

What stood out to me in this reading: _____

_____

_____

_____

_____

How I can praise God and be a better Christian today and tomorrow:

_____

_____

Things God has laid on my heart today:

_____

_____

I praise You God for my eyes, my ears, my mouth, my mind, my hands and my feet.

What I'm most grateful for today:

_____

Lord, help me tomorrow to:

_____

My spiritual goal this week:

_____

Date _____

Prayer Prompter: **Dear Father, thank You for forgiving and forgetting my every sin.**

Friends I need to pray for:

_____   _____   _____

_____   _____   _____

Things on my heart:

_____   _____   _____

Answers to prayer:

_____

_____

Personal requests:

_____

_____

Today's Scripture reading (up to me): _____

What stood out to me in this reading: _____

_____

_____

_____

_____

How I can praise God and be a better Christian today and tomorrow:

_____

_____

Things God has laid on my heart today:

_____

_____

Lord, help me be a Christian who is a good example.

What I'm most grateful for today:

_____

Lord, help me tomorrow to:

_____

My spiritual goal this week:

_____

Date _____

Prayer Prompter: **Dear Lord, quiet my mind and steady my hurried pace.**

Friends I need to pray for:

_____   _____   _____

_____   _____   _____

Things on my heart:

_____   _____   _____

Answers to prayer:

_____

_____

Personal requests:

_____

_____

Today's Scripture reading (up to me): _____

What stood out to me in this reading: _____

_____

_____

_____

_____

How I can praise God and be a better Christian today and tomorrow:

_____

_____

Things God has laid on my heart today:

_____

_____

I praise you, my Father, for another day, week, and month.

What I'm most grateful for today:

_____

Lord, help me tomorrow to:

_____

My spiritual goal this week:

_____

Date _____

Prayer Prompter: **Dear Lord, thank You for looking beyond my faults.**

Friends I need to pray for:

_____   _____   _____

_____   _____   _____

Things on my heart:

_____   _____   _____

Answers to prayer:

_____

_____

Personal requests:

_____

_____

_____

Today's Scripture reading (up to me): _____

What stood out to me in this reading: _____

_____

_____

_____

_____

How I can praise God and be a better Christian today and tomorrow:

_____

_____

Things God has laid on my heart today:

_____

_____

Dear Jesus, thank You.

What I'm most grateful for today:

_____

Lord, help me tomorrow to:

_____

My spiritual goal this week:

_____

Date _____

Prayer Prompter: **Dear Lord, thank You for loving me unconditionally.**

Friends I need to pray for:

_____   _____   _____

_____   _____   _____

Things on my heart:

_____   _____   _____

Answers to prayer:

_____

_____

Personal requests:

_____

_____

Today's Scripture reading (up to me): _____

What stood out to me in this reading: _____

_____

_____

_____

_____

How I can praise God and be a better Christian today and tomorrow:

_____

_____

Things God has laid on my heart today:

_____

_____

I praise You God for the bad as well as the good.

What I'm most grateful for today:

_____

Lord, help me tomorrow to:

_____

My spiritual goal this week:

_____

Date _____

Prayer Prompter: **Dear Lord, direct my thoughts and actions today.**

Friends I need to pray for:

_____   _____   _____

_____   _____   _____

Things on my heart:

_____   _____   _____

Answers to prayer:

_____

_____

Personal requests:

_____

_____

_____

Today's Scripture reading (up to me): _____

What stood out to me in this reading: _____

_____

_____

_____

_____

How I can praise God and be a better Christian today and tomorrow:

_____

_____

Things God has laid on my heart today:

_____

_____

Lord, only You know the perfect reason why bad things happen. Help me trust You.

What I'm most grateful for today:

_____

Lord, help me tomorrow to:

_____

My spiritual goal this week:

_____

Date _____

Prayer Prompter: **Dear Heavenly Father, thank You that in Christ I'm chosen.**

Friends I need to pray for:

_____   _____   _____

_____   _____   _____

Things on my heart:

_____   _____   _____

Answers to prayer:

_____

_____

Personal requests:

_____

_____

Today's Scripture reading (up to me): _____

What stood out to me in this reading: _____

_____

_____

_____

_____

How I can praise God and be a better Christian today and tomorrow:

_____

_____

Things God has laid on my heart today:

_____

_____

Lord, thank You for taking my burdens.

What I'm most grateful for today:

_____

Lord, help me tomorrow to:

_____

My spiritual goal this week:

_____

Date _____

Prayer Prompter: **Dear Lord, You are my only hope. Thank You.**

Friends I need to pray for:

_____   _____   _____

_____   _____   _____

Things on my heart:

_____   _____   _____

Answers to prayer:

_____

_____

Personal requests:

_____

_____

Today's Scripture reading (up to me): _____

What stood out to me in this reading: _____

_____

_____

_____

_____

How I can praise God and be a better Christian today and tomorrow:

_____

_____

Things God has laid on my heart today:

_____

_____

I thank You God for listening to my problems.

What I'm most grateful for today:

_____

Lord, help me tomorrow to:

_____

My spiritual goal this week:

_____

Date _____

Prayer Prompter: **Dear Lord, I'm sorry for my complaints.**

Friends I need to pray for:

_____   _____   _____

_____   _____   _____

Things on my heart:

_____   _____   _____

Answers to prayer:

_____

_____

Personal requests:

_____

_____

Today's Scripture reading (up to me): _____

What stood out to me in this reading: _____

_____

_____

_____

_____

How I can praise God and be a better Christian today and tomorrow:

_____

_____

Things God has laid on my heart today:

_____

_____

I praise You God. Have mercy on me.

What I'm most grateful for today:

_____

Lord, help me tomorrow to:

_____

My spiritual goal this week:

_____

Date _____

Prayer Prompter: **Dear Lord, please forgive me for my bad attitude.**

Friends I need to pray for:

_____   _____   _____

_____   _____   _____

Things on my heart:

_____   _____   _____

Answers to prayer:

_____

_____

Personal requests:

_____

_____

Today's Scripture reading (up to me): _____

What stood out to me in this reading: _____

_____

_____

_____

_____

How I can praise God and be a better Christian today and tomorrow:

_____

_____

Things God has laid on my heart today:

_____

_____

_____

I praise You God, the Author of the universe, the Creator of all things.

What I'm most grateful for today:

_____

Lord, help me tomorrow to:

_____

My spiritual goal this week:

_____

Date _____

Prayer Prompter: **Dear God, I see Your hand at work. Let me be a part of it.**

Friends I need to pray for:

_____   _____   _____

_____   _____   _____

Things on my heart:

_____   _____   _____

Answers to prayer:

_____

_____

Personal requests:

_____

_____

Today's Scripture reading (up to me): _____

What stood out to me in this reading: _____

_____

_____

_____

_____

How I can praise God and be a better Christian today and tomorrow:

_____

_____

Things God has laid on my heart today:

_____

_____

Thank You for forgiving my sins and forgetting them.

What I'm most grateful for today:

_____

Lord, help me tomorrow to:

_____

My spiritual goal this week:

_____

Date _____

Prayer Prompter: **Dear Lord, help me live a life that proclaims Your excellence.**

Friends I need to pray for:

_____   _____   _____

_____   _____   _____

Things on my heart:

_____   _____   _____

Answers to prayer:

_____

_____

Personal requests:

_____

_____

Today's Scripture reading (up to me): _____

What stood out to me in this reading: _____

_____

_____

_____

_____

How I can praise God and be a better Christian today and tomorrow:

_____

_____

Things God has laid on my heart today:

_____

_____

Dear Lord, help me forgive others.

What I'm most grateful for today:

_____

Lord, help me tomorrow to:

_____

My spiritual goal this week:

_____

Date _____

Prayer Prompter: **Dear Lord, open my eyes to the gifts You've given me.**

Friends I need to pray for:

_____   _____   _____

_____   _____   _____

Things on my heart:

_____   _____   _____

Answers to prayer:

_____

_____

Personal requests:

_____

_____

Today's Scripture reading (up to me): _____

What stood out to me in this reading: _____

_____

_____

_____

_____

How I can praise God and be a better Christian today and tomorrow:

_____

_____

Things God has laid on my heart today:

_____

_____

Father God, help me love others who are hard to like.

What I'm most grateful for today:

_____

Lord, help me tomorrow to:

_____

My spiritual goal this week:

_____

Date _____

Prayer Prompter: **Dear Lord, thank You for sending Jesus to save me.**

Friends I need to pray for:

_____   _____   _____

_____   _____   _____

Things on my heart:

_____   _____   _____

Answers to prayer:

_____

_____

Personal requests:

_____

_____

_____

Today's Scripture reading (up to me): _____

What stood out to me in this reading: _____

_____

_____

_____

_____

How I can praise God and be a better Christian today and tomorrow:

_____

_____

Things God has laid on my heart today:

_____

_____

Thank You Lord for putting _____ in my life.

What I'm most grateful for today:

_____

Lord, help me tomorrow to:

_____

My spiritual goal this week:

_____

Date _____

Prayer Prompter: **Dear Lord, thank You for being with me in my sorrows.**

Friends I need to pray for:

_____   _____   _____

_____   _____   _____

Things on my heart:

_____   _____   _____

Answers to prayer:

_____

_____

Personal requests:

_____

_____

Today's Scripture reading (up to me): _____

What stood out to me in this reading: _____

_____

_____

_____

_____

How I can praise God and be a better Christian today and tomorrow:

_____

_____

Things God has laid on my heart today:

_____

_____

I praise You Jesus. You are the way, the truth, and the life.

What I'm most grateful for today:

_____

Lord, help me tomorrow to:

_____

My spiritual goal this week:

_____

Date _____

Prayer Prompter: **Dear Lord, I thank You for Your greatness.**

Friends I need to pray for:

_____   _____   _____

_____   _____   _____

Things on my heart:

_____   _____   _____

Answers to prayer:

_____

_____

Personal requests:

_____

_____

_____

Today's Scripture reading (up to me): _____

What stood out to me in this reading: _____

_____

_____

_____

_____

How I can praise God and be a better Christian today and tomorrow:

_____

_____

Things God has laid on my heart today:

_____

_____

_____

I praise You God for answering my prayers. Help me trust You more.

What I'm most grateful for today:

_____

Lord, help me tomorrow to:

_____

My spiritual goal this week:

_____

Date _____

Prayer Prompter: **Dear Almighty God, give me a measure of Your strength today.**

Friends I need to pray for:

_____   _____   _____

_____   _____   _____

Things on my heart:

_____   _____   _____

Answers to prayer:

_____

_____

Personal requests:

_____

_____

_____

Today's Scripture reading (up to me): _____

What stood out to me in this reading: _____

_____

_____

_____

_____

How I can praise God and be a better Christian today and tomorrow:

_____

_____

Things God has laid on my heart today:

_____

_____

Lord, lift my spirit when I am weak.

What I'm most grateful for today:

_____

Lord, help me tomorrow to:

_____

My spiritual goal this week:

_____

Date _____

Prayer Prompter: **Dear Lord, help me honor You in all I do today.**

Friends I need to pray for:

_____   _____   _____

_____   _____   _____

Things on my heart:

_____   _____   _____

Answers to prayer:

_____

_____

Personal requests:

_____

_____

Today's Scripture reading (up to me): _____

What stood out to me in this reading: _____

_____

_____

_____

_____

How I can praise God and be a better Christian today and tomorrow:

_____

_____

Things God has laid on my heart today:

_____

_____

Dear Father, thank You for keeping me safe from unseen evil.

What I'm most grateful for today:

_____

Lord, help me tomorrow to:

_____

My spiritual goal this week:

_____

Date _____

Prayer Prompter: **Dear Lord, help me not give in to discouragement, deception, or doubt.**

Friends I need to pray for:

_____   _____   _____

_____   _____   _____

Things on my heart:

_____   _____   _____

Answers to prayer:

_____

_____

Personal requests:

_____

_____

Today's Scripture reading (up to me): _____

What stood out to me in this reading: _____

_____

_____

_____

_____

How I can praise God and be a better Christian today and tomorrow:

_____

_____

Things God has laid on my heart today:

_____

_____

All good things come from You, Lord. Thank You.

What I'm most grateful for today:

_____

Lord, help me tomorrow to:

_____

My spiritual goal this week:

_____

Date _____

Prayer Prompter: **Dear Father, be with me every hour of this day. Thank You.**

Friends I need to pray for:

_____   _____   _____

_____   _____   _____

Things on my heart:

_____   _____   _____

Answers to prayer:

_____

_____

Personal requests:

_____

_____

Today's Scripture reading (up to me): _____

What stood out to me in this reading: _____

_____

_____

_____

_____

How I can praise God and be a better Christian today and tomorrow:

_____

_____

Things God has laid on my heart today:

_____

_____

Lord, bless all who study Your Word and pray to You. Bless those who finish this workbook.

Books by Debra Chapoton

Christian Cowboy Romance:
Tangled in Fate's Reins
Rodeo Romance
A Cowboy's Promise
Heartstrings and Horseshoes
Kisses at Sundown
Montana Heaven
Montana Moments
Tamed Heart
Wrangler's Embrace
Moonlight and Spurs
Whispers on the Range
Christmas at the Double Horseshoe Ranch

Scottish Romance
The Highlander's Secret Princess
The Highlander's English Maiden
The Highlander's Hidden Castle
The Highlander's Heart of Stone
The Highlander's Forbidden Love

Second Chance Teacher Romance series
written under pen name Marlisa Kriscott
(Christian themes):

Aaron After School
Sonia's Secret Someone
Melanie's Match
School's Out
Summer School
The Spanish Tutor
A Novel Thing

Christian Non-fiction:
Guided Prayer Journal for Women
Crossing the Scriptures
35 Lessons from the Book of Psalms
Prayer Journal and Bible Study (general)
Prayer Journal and Bible Study in the Gospels
Teens in the Bible
Moms in the Bible
Animals in the Bible
Old Testament Lessons in the Bible
New Testament Lessons in the Bible

Christian Fiction:
Love Contained
Sheltered
The Guardian's Diary
Exodia
Out of Exodia
Spell of the Shadow Dragon
Curse of the Winter Dragon

Young Adult Novels:
A Soul's Kiss
Edge of Escape
Exodia
Out of Exodia
Here Without a Trace
Sheltered
Spell of the Shadow Dragon
Curse of the Winter Dragon
The Girl in the Time Machine
The Guardian's Diary
The Time Bender
The Time Ender
The Time Pacer
The Time Stopper
To Die Upon a Kiss
A Fault of Graves

Children's Books:
The Secret in the Hidden Cave
Mystery's Grave
Bullies and Bears
A Tick in Time
Bigfoot Day, Ninja Night
Nick Bazebahl and Forbidden Tunnels
Nick Bazebahl and the Cartoon Tunnels
Nick Bazebahl and the Fake Witch Tunnels
Nick Bazebahl and the Mining Tunnels
Nick Bazebahl and the Red Tunnels
Nick Bazebahl and the Wormhole Tunnels
Inspirational Bible Verse Coloring Book
ABC Learn to Read Coloring Book
ABC Learn to Read Spanish Coloring Book
Stained Glass Window Coloring Book
Naughty Cat Dotted Grid Notebook
Cute Puppy Graph Paper Notebook
Easy Sudoku for Kids
101 Mandalas Coloring Book
150 Mandalas Coloring Book
Whimsical Cat Mandalas Coloring Book

Non-Fiction:
Brain Power Puzzles (11 volumes)
Building a Log Home in Under a Year
200 Creative Writing Prompts
400 Creative Writing Prompts
Advanced Creative Writing Prompts
Beyond Creative Writing Prompts
300 Plus Teacher Hacks and Tips
How to Blend Families
How to Help Your Child Succeed in School
How to Teach a Foreign Language

Early Readers

The Kindness Parade, The Caring Kids: Spreading Kindness Everywhere

The Colors of Friendship: The Caring Kids, Embracing Diversity

Believe In Yourself, The Caring Kids: Building Self Esteem

Friends With Fur and Feathers: The Caring Kids, Animal Friends

Celebrations All Year Round: The Caring Kids: Our Special Days

Feelings in Full Color: The Caring Kids: A Guide to Feelings

Made in United States
Cleveland, OH
17 November 2024

10710472R10103